POOLS OF GOLD

Poems by

John Barton Watson

Illustrated by Walter Parker

1st Edition September 2005

ISBN: 0-9550686-0-6

web site: www.poolsofgold.com

email: jbw@assureweb.com

Printed by
Ashford Colour Press Ltd.
Gosport, Hampshire

Forward
by
Rt Hon William Hague MP

This delightful collection of poems by John Watson, with charming illustrations by Walter Parker, captures the very essence of North Yorkshire: the spirit of her people, the splendour of her buildings and the beauty of her countryside.

From poignant memories of his childhood to simple observations of daily life, this compilation is both stirring and tender.

I challenge any reader not to be touched and uplifted by this book.

William Hague

The Rt Hon William Hague MP
May 2005

ACKNOWLEDGMENTS

Firstly I would like to thank Mick and Judy Norman for their encouragement in first persuading me to consider compiling my poetry into a book.

Also to Paul and Jane Thompson for their interest, support and advice and the invaluable help of my family and friends.

To The Rt. Hon William Hague MP, my thanks for his kind words and consideration.

Finally my thanks go to Walter Parker to whom I am eternally grateful for his superb and sympathetic watercolour illustrations which complement and bring to life each poem.

John Barton Watson.   September 2005

CONTENTS

DAWN

Still,
Whilst people sleep
The earth awakes
From night's
Cold fast of light
To tempt the Sun's
Candescent rays
And burn away
The misty white
Of dawn's first breath
To quench each leaf
Of plants and trees baptised
By Nature's hand.
The gift of life
To passive earth commend.

THE DOVECOTE

Facing every way at once
My sanguine-coloured skin
That looked for centuries
Upon the flapping sails of lazy boats
Through daybreak mists
And leaden skies
To watch the peaceful river's silent flow
And busy children fishing
From smelly skinyard walls
That once the loading ships brushed sides
And later carcasses passed by
On slow tides high and low.
A ghost wherein a Stockton street
My predecessor lies.

Forged by man's terrestrial hand
From Earth's riparian crust
To mould a hive
Of biblical design
My selfish Ark
Took only one of many kind.
But now in temporal decline
Such symbiotic guests
That once for peace
Were but a sign
In stately coliseum lined
Desert each tenemented suite
And so no hope have I,
But time.

AN IRISH WELCOME

When friends offer you
  their home,
And give up within it
  their own space.

When they provide all the
  meals you need,
And care for your every want
  with courtesy and grace.

When they open their
  hearts to you,
And share the way
  they live,

Then that friendship
  must be cherished
For there's no more
  they can give.

THE WAITING ROOM

Expressions, complexions
  Thin, drawn and pale,
Shapes of all sizes,
  Fat, plump and frail.
Decrepit old timepiece
  Clutching the wall
And roughly each hour
  You can hear it call
'The Nell' of anxiety
  In uncertain air,
The twitching of fingers,
  The twirling of hair,
The crackle of magazines,
  The shuffling of feet,
Legs crossed and crooked
  And eyes that look weak.
Noses like branches
  That bend under strain,
People who whistle
  Quietly in vain.
People who worry
  With the hour they spend
On the visit to the surgery
  And our medical friend.

OXBRIDGE SCHOOL
AND THEREABOUTS

Jangling change in pockets rang
The knell of abject fear,
And spitting forth from 6'-6"
The Head sent showers near.

And from his lofty eminence
This tyrant ruled the school,
His captives never questioned
The captor's Spartan rule.

The glass and wood partitions
And brick-floored corridors,
The smell of coffee boiling
The staffroom's welcome chores.

Simple wooden desk tops
With white ceramic wells,
To scratch and blotch your learning day
With black ink-covered quills.

The playground and the red-brick walls
And Marlborough's corner shop,
A Venus fly trap of delight
For children's hungry stop.

Adventure that was Ropner Park,
The birds' nests and the lake,
The aviary and the teapot lid
My spinning head to ache.

Catching fish you could not eat
Or newts you could not keep,
Taking duck eggs home to fry.
The Bricky waters deep.

The Homes' kids and their leather boots
Amorphous woolly clothes,
No parents these for arms to hold
And feel forever close.

The No.4 I used to race
From school to Preston Road.
Pass it at each busy stop
And breathless reach my goal.

Making slides on Lustrum Beck
In deepest winter's hold,
When ice would lock for weeks on end
Your freedom's door, by cold.

Caterpillars and Cabbage Whites
A summer's garden treat,
Jam jars full of frogspawn soup
A sago not to eat.

The owl's penumbral eerie shape
In Green Lane's ivy trees,
Its ghost in twilight's darkness looms
A child's quick step to freeze.

Memories now seem distant dreams
Of playgrounds, parks and fields,
Of meadow-scented waving grass
And butterflies and streams.

Of these my earliest days so rich
A treasure none can steal,
Such mnemonistic happenings keep
My dreams forever real.

GIRSBY SUNSET

Before me patterned fields are spread
Neath a wild September sky
O'er silhouettes of trees for miles
The clouds go racing by.

The crimson and the blue and grey
The violet violent shapes
The low clouds outpace the high
As past the hill top scrapes.

The cattle in the valley graze
Amid the thistled grass
Black and white their coats stand out
As daytime darkness casts.

For soon the mirror river
Reflecting dusk's last light
Will swallow up the sunset
And leave us naught, but night.

THE CHURCHYARD

Where are they now?
These people
Blessed of man's earthly spirit.

A thousand autumns
Now have passed
Since first the hallowed stone was cast
And leave their earthly bodies last
Amid the soil
To join beloved kindred souls
And death to foil.

Where are they now?
To watch us
Tend the ground they left
And clear the moss
And golden leaves
To find a name
No longer for a mortal heart to grieve.

Where are they now?
Raised from this secret garden
That is Nature's own domain
And though we trim the edges round
With Nature it remains
To know their final resting place
Where life was just a dream.

Where are they now?
Those who had not known love.
Will they be loved?
Those incarnate sorrowed
Be healed of pain
Will those who's way was lost
Find their path again?

Where are they now?

9

KATIE

Katie, bonny Katie
With laughing eyes so bright
You bring the warmth of sunshine
When life is not so light.
You're a diamond in the afternoon
But a jade sometimes at night.
Katie, bonny Katie.

When people visit they have tried,
But none can match your rising tide
Of zestful life you never hide.
You keep us fully occupied
By day and night and more besides.
The flow is never ending.

Katie, bonny Katie
You're mischief all the while
When neighbours or relations call
Of them you soon beguile.
When daddy says "You little scamp"
You just look up and smile,
Katie, bonny Katie.

In years to come
When life's long day is nearing its close,
When you have gone,
And married life's the path that you have chose,
The memories that fill our hearts
Will be forever close.
Katie, bonny Katie.

THE MOAT FIELD

The bustle of the day is just a memory now
  and all around me life is slowing down.
The sound of church bells long have died away
  and darkness soon will be a covering gown.

But in the dying light I feel the slightest breeze
  a chance to smell the honeysuckle's scent
And moths to see its pollen thieve,
  a chance to see an early fox
Through hay bales dodge and weave,
  a chance, maybe, to catch a vole,
For cubs have hungry mouths to feed.

The setting sun has long since gone.
  Through crimson shafts I still behold
The slender reeds no longer show a saffron tint
  but whisper of the secrets night will hold.
Now only silhouettes remain
  all colours lose their magic flair,
Bats like butterflies reel and turn
  and lend enchantment to the evening air.

Everything to the eye is lost
  as darkness is but everywhere.
My thoughts go to my father past
  With whom these times I often shared.
And now in stillness
  cold and dark abounds
Blending the moonless sky and ground,
  summer night's fragrance fills the air
The blackness etched with spidery sounds.

A barking sheepdog guards a distant home
  a day has once more reached its end, and gone.

11

HIGH TEES

Born in purple heathered bells
A land that ice once gripped
And carved the shapes
Of rolling hills
To skyward lift
Frondescent turf
With forest trees
To brush the passing clouds
And make eternal life
Pour down on valleys such as these.
By force to push
Through yawning rocks
And plunge the depths
Of black water stained by peat
That holds beneath a mystery
Of the deep
Where trout and even salmon lie
Beneath the beech trees
Clinging to the granite's set
That when in autumn's wake
Drop leaves of red and gold
To settle on a mirror
Black as jet
And float like paper boats
Towards a cold sea.
Past alpine plants
And meadows
Cropped by famished sheep
Through fields
The course of which
A myriad of villages pass
Cosseted and dependent cling
And nurtured as a queen of bees
Each fireside, homestead, hamlet
Tower and town,
Dependent on its life are these.

When Roman feet
And armies crossed its fords
On golden shingled pebbled stones
And later kings and horsemen
Stopped to drink
Through shimmering reflections
And built their castles, roads and homes
Within its sound
Where conscience
No man dutifully bound
Devolved through generations
Such sacramental faith
To build a history
By the river's ground.

THE TASK

A spirit appeared from Heaven
  And asked of a scientist true
To build him a bird.
  Any species at all.
In fact, any bird he chooses to do.
  "I'll do that," said the scientist
"And for ease, I'll choose the wren.
  What time do we have to complete this task?"
Said the spirit, "In 1000 years I'll return".

After this, sempiternal scheme
  The spirit appeared again
To find the task was finally complete,
  That the work had not been in vain.

"It can walk and fly"
  Said the scientist.
Proud of what history could bring.
  Said the spirit, "In 10,000 years I'll return
See if you can get it to sing".

DREAMS

Halls and rooms you think you see
But know you've never been

Places where you think you are
But know you cannot be

People you think you're with
But know you'll never see

Within the arms of Morpheus
But know you'll not be free

Until the Dogs of Daylight
Let slip reality.

15

THE DARKEST SUNDAY

This April evening
Whilst the birds are singing
Light rain falls fresh and clean.

Do not rejoice
As you would when life this season
Springs so fresh and green.

Do not smile
And be joyful for the vista rich
Is but an empty scene.

Do not listen,
For the lambs and sheep have gone
And deafening silence fills the fields
Where they have been.

KEEP OUT
FOOT
AND MOUTH

A WINTER'S SCENE

When winter strikes its seasoned fangs
Of devilment through clouds and hangs
Its stormy burden hovering mass
To empty on the greyness cast
The landscape locked in stillness as
A winter's scene.
A snowy picture waits the brush
A canvas clean before the flush.
Shafts of sunlight cast a spell
Illuminate the distant fell.
But still the mounting tension grows
As feeling of the stillness shows
In contrast twixt
The sunlight and the darkness mixed
For all to see.
A barren beauty lost of green
Its death, the life, of winter's scene.

DEIGHTON CHURCH

Still stands the chapel that for centuries
  has worn the shawl of age.
The bells that ring a timeless knell
  the villagers to page.
Through stained glass panes
  you watch so close the village life go by
Some visitors who come to pray
  and some who come to lie.

Each in his tomb of endless time
  forever there to lay
With just a lichen-covered stone
  to mark the year and day.
But weather's hand will slowly wear
  the last remaining sign
To say that they in Deighton lived
  or did nearby reside.

Within your womb of slated roof
  and ivy-covered walls
The history of a parish
  has evolved around your calls.
Horse-drawn feudal landlords
  and horse-drawn ploughs that scrape
A pattern on the countryside
  a living in their wake.

Within your shadow bricks and tiles
  indigenously made,
Have formed the dwellings that surround
  your pastoral landscape.
Though times have changed in passing years
  It's nature's ceaseless face
That holds the beauty of this church
  this place of prayer and grace.

Chapel of ease, your Galilee
  has watched in by-gone years
The children in the schoolhouse near
  the laughter and the tears.
You've heard the village smithy
  mending horse's tired feet
The banging of the anvil
  the bellows blowing heat.

You keep that time locked secret
  that's forever yours to hold
The mystery of the village moat
  that enigma of the fold.
A flat raised field where history hides
  and only cattle graze
You hold the key, both then and now
  to the community you gaze.

So long may you stand for summer's hand
  to bring the swallows nye
To swoop around your sandstone walls
  and through your belfry fly
To see that golden carpet, Autumn's leafy shroud to lay
  to see the soundless whiteness,
Of an early winter's day.

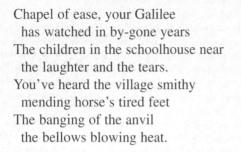

THE CENOTAPH

Heads bowed
we listen to their names
and think
how far away they are.
Their own aphelion
measured by eternity.
Can they hear us now
these souls
brave once
but now too far away.
How can they hear
the words we say
When no one heard the Robin sing.

SWANS

Church pews fill
With Sunday morning people
And sunlight from the open door.
Footsteps all around me fall
On ancient stone-flagged floors.

Where are you?
I can never find you,
Though every time I search,
They say that you're beside me
In your house that is this church.

Is the answer
With the song thrush
That sang the sermon through
And filled the hallowed vaulted rooms
With stanzas clear and true?

Or in the fields
And mountain streams
And woodlands far and wide,
Or in amongst these sandstone walls
Where graceful swans do glide?

THE POACHER

A wanton fellow
  Of waste and need,
His nerves of steel
  His heart of greed,
Creeps out in the night
  When there's half a moon,
His blasphemous deeds
  Soon to be strewn.
Across the fields and o'er the dale
  While the gillies and gentry
Are supping their ale.

He's out in the moonlight
  In his old grey coat
Fancy clothes for himself
  He will nae devote.
There's too many uses
  For his old grey coat.

Now into the wood
  There's a wind blowing hard,
But that's all part
  Of this deadly charade.
If nerves you have none
  Then there's naught I can say
But to put aside
  This dangerous game
And find your own means
  Where there's no refrain.

He looks through the trees
  With experienced eye
A shape or some outline
  To identify.
Like the pheasant bold
  With its long hanging tail
An important shape
  In this night,
In this tale.

Reaching out
  With a loop on a stick
He throttles the pheasant
  And hard it does kick
And flap and flutter
  And fight to the end,
But it matters least
  To our poacher friend,
For the wind on this night
  Will conceal his dark deeds,
It will hide his misdoings
  By shaking the trees,
Backwards and forward
  And side by side,
In a wood that's alive
  An intruder can hide.

So down the hedgerows
  You'll see him creep
Setting his snares
  And nets to reap
Hares, rabbits and partridges fine
  And whate'er he can find
In this night sublime.

His sack's much heavier
  And harder to hold
Dogs are barking quite near
  The night's getting cold.
Quick, back to the house
  Before it's too late
There's no time to lose
  In this growing spate
Of curious people
  In the farmhouse near,
There's suspicions aroused
  By a sentry to fear
So he hurries along
  With his bag so fine
To the household,
  To safety,
To peace of mind.

When he opens the door
  It's quiet within
And there's no need to tell
  A soul where he's been
With the game in the larder
  And the fire so bright,
He can rest in the armchair
  And dream of some night
When once again
  The fruit he will pick
From the trees
  From the fields
From the hedgerows thick.

COVERDALE FELLS

On Witton's lonely fell I stand
To wonder at the Vista drawn
By earth's volcanic hand.
That brewed the leavens substance formed
And shaped this warrened land.

When glory ran from sword to shield,
And castles touched the sky,
When streams ran blood and lances called,
The holder's right to go and live
Or else to stay and die.

Now peace has filled these heathered hills
Since Vikings dynast swathe,
Left Caldbergh's denizen settlement
To cling upon the hillside ling
These pirates of the waves.

LONELINESS

I'm here again
Too early to start the day
Walking down the Castle's steepest path
And listen to the river say,
I'm too early to start the day.

The ducks are here again
They splash and swim and stare.
Creamy foam beneath black rocks
Upon the darkest of the deepest pools.
Is the answer there?

Rooks and jackdaws throng
To fill the tops of empty trees
And weave their homes
Amongst the flotsam sticks and leaves.
No care for hope have these.

I'm here again
To escape from arriving alone, this way.
The emptiness I've come to bear
And all the time knowing
I'm too early to start the day.

25

THE OLD VILLAGE HALL

Painted green
It's stood here now
Some twenty years and seventeen.
With shaky walls
And bendy floor
And iron sneck upon the door
As teapots brim
To overflow
Its life's been full to bursting.

The green baize tables
Spread about
Have drawn
Our distant neighbours.
A game to worship as devout,
A following unsurpassed
No doubt,
A congregation drawn till now
Have been both guests
And saviours.

But now the end
Is drawing nigh
The creaking floor
Will bend a sigh
To take the last strained
Party's cry
The bustle and the noise
Will fall.
The domino tables'
Final call
The shuffles like skeleton bones
And all
Amid the Autumn Wake
Where once, a friendly building stood
Another, we must make.

THE CHRISTMAS CARD

Courage sometimes dormant lies
Beneath the cloak of fear
To surface through a tremulous hand
A special Christmas cheer.

The crusty door's incumbent host
Took forth the humble card
The greatest story ever told
Was once again, The Star.

SCARBOROUGH MEMORIES

The windmill's last quixotic stand
Passed many years ago
No longer by the miller's hand
The salt wind sails to blow.

Below the cloistered bricks and tiles
And roofs and chimneys red,
The claustrophobic streets have dried
Its life stream's stony bed.

Its rigored arms in working life
Turned wheat seeds into flour
Kindness would its burial be
To seal that final hour.

To shops and stores and seaplace fronts
The windmill spreads its pall,
An effigy to life long past
My childhood memories call.

A dinosaur of modern times
Stands high above the town
To view through eyes of dusty grime
And red Victorian gown,

A bay that was the country's best
With railings black and gold,
The pleasure boats and fish quay stalls
Drew people to its fold.

But still exciting are the gaps
Of hotels looking through
Where just beyond their painted walls
The sea lies wide and blue.

Upon the vetche's table cloth
A top the lofty cliffs,
The ancient castle's skeleton
Surveys the distant ships.

The screaming of the kittiwakes,
The smell of diesel brine,
A walk along the harbour wall,
The spinning floss divine.

No better seat had Claudius
Than Holmcliff's weekly lease,
The hallowed cricket ground to view
The gladiator's crease.

Thunder as the rough sea waves
Pound promenades below
With spray clouds sixty feet or more
Leave jetsam far ashore.

And last the toys in coloured shops
The fishing nets and canes
The hissing of the Peasholm train
And battleships and planes.

The putting greens, the North Bay Pool
My double-barrelled gun,
The coloured shops of sweets and toys
Have lost their magic fun.

But still the memories and days of joy
And hired car I see
Mam and Dad and Uncle Joe and Auntie Eth,
And me.

29

MESSAGE FROM THE GODS

Sweat comes too easily now
And limbs ache sooner.
Fells are steeper
But you cannot
Run on memories
Or pretend your body's younger.

Once I glided
High above the clouds
As if on air
From top to top
As if my feet had wings
For Hermes to compare.

But now I see
What I did not see before.
A chaffinch nest
In winter's open hedge
Where once the summer leaves
Concealed the brooding bird and eggs.

More time to think,
Though not enough besotted
By infliction of defeat
To smell the flowers,
And heady scent of bog myrtle
Crushed beneath my feet.

EXTEMPORE HELP

Sometimes you need a helping hand
To cross the road of life
When dreams and aspirations fail
And daytime seems but night

Then love from an unlikely source
A strong arm there to give
Leaves the carer and the cared for left,
The better for the gift.

LIFE AFTER LIFE

When life is cast
A time that's spanned
Immeasurably small
Of being in a living land
What will transition be
If not by some unearthly hand
That takes the cradled burning soul
To gather on the border's path
And cross into another world
To quench the mystery
Of a million years
Where eternity rewards
All whose patience
Faith bestowed.

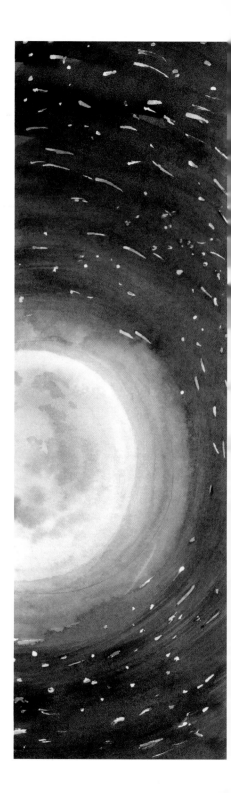

GOODBYE

Goodbye Freda.
I saw you lying,
Your hair was white and fluffy
As it was the day before.
You looked so peaceful.

But once again I was too late
To say goodbye,
And it's fish day tomorrow
But I won't go to the stall.

You'll remember our formula;
For "this 'ere" and "that there"
The difference only we can share.

I'll toll the bell
To say goodbye
And know you will not mind
How well,
But just that it's I
Who tolls the bell.

THE BORDER REIVERS

The Armstrongs and the Eliots too
The Cessford Kerrs and Scotts
The Crosers and the Nixon clan
Their lives a looting plot

These riding names allegiance had
To no one but their own
The Bells and Fenwicks, Forsters clan
Their homes to guard alone

When Hadrian built his stony wedge
To break a nation's soul
It may have worked when first it formed
But only came to show

Another world of war and death
And vicious looting raids
The force of fear when moon's grey light
Was life the price to sate

Beware of autumn's early frosts
The hardened ground to take
Plundered livestock, sheep and beasts
And murder in their wake

For when the moon is full and white
And snow lies thick and deep
And night time turns itself to day
And men and horses creep

Torpid bees in dark walls sleep
And salmon cut their redds
When corbies roost in branches bare
And man lays warm in bed

Then nightmares turn from sleep to sight
As from the Bastle walls
The beacons roar and people scream
As hobblers snorting calls

Muffled by the midnight snow
The galloway's fearsome mount
"Steill" bonneted with "Jak"and Stave
Their raid in blood to count

For in retreat they'd sack and "spoyl"
And pillage farms and land
A rear guard was left to warn
A posse was at hand

The "Hot Trod" route was filled with fear
As careful traps were laid
To ambush riders in pursuit
And take their lives to pay

The Kings and Queens our nations both
Before their crowns were one
Did separate the border land
In Marches from the Wall

Each March was by a Warden' s hand
Ruled with ruthless greed
From Kershopefoot and Annandale
To Berwick-upon-Tweed

These tyrants under rule of law
A blind eye oft did turn
To raids and siege and "scumfishing"
The Pele rooms set to burn

And then the days of Truce came round
A reckoning of the rogues
A time to dress in finery
If you weren't due for the rope

Each Warden's tent was pitched upon
The frosty winter's field
Two hundred of his best armed men
Would vow his life to shield

When shiny metal armour clinked
And nervous horses bayed and jinked
With snorting breath in frosty air
Their riders armed with lances stare
Across the Kershopeburn they glare
But dare not go

As plaintiffs and defendants care
To stand their ground
The Warden's final word to spare
Or prison bound

And having read the parchment scrolls
Of wanted, broken men
Of Bells and Burns and Taits and Potts
Of who killed what, and when

The armed men leave the Day of Truce
To reach their homes again
Some to cross the Tarras Moss
And some the Solway plain

Sound sleep at night was nae to be
When days were short and dark
And watching eyes from hills beyond
Planned terror cold and stark

When riders' spurs on dinner plates
Set plans afoot once more
To raid your neighbour's livelihood
And fill the empty store

When night and ground became as one
A wilderness to cross
The smell of leather damp with dew
In peat bogs sphagnum moss

Unless a blackmail toll you paid
To Armstrongs or the Grahams
Your Pele or Bastle "yett" they'd break
And kill your wife and weans

Castles come and castles go
But nowhere in this land
Could match the dark foreboding
Of the Heritage's stand

This cockpit of the reivers' world
A special Warden's seat
So he controlled and lived within
This awesome Liddle Keep

Complicity was ever rife
With the Keeper and the kept
The cosy pact with Kinmont's men
And the Eliots' devious sept

The Queen of Scots once rode non-stop
To tend her wounded love
From Edinburgh to Hermitage
For Bothwell's life betroth

But border clans would vacillate
From English into Scots
And at a stroke they'd change again
To leave their Queen to rot

So Mary's long decline began
On Leven's island home
And force her there to abdicate
Her way of life and throne

The sands of raid and deadly feud
Were running very low
Soon after Mary lost her head
The borderers' path was closed

No more will beams of sunlight glint
Or bright the cresset's bowl
Illuminate the shiny spurs
And Spanish Morion's comb

The Moss Troopers were last to go
Whilst moon and moors were theirs
But "Jeddart Justice" did for them
What James did for their peers

And so this life passed into time
Of history's tarnished rose
The "Last Goodnight" had come and gone
The final chapter closed

Now when in Cheviots hills you roam
Or Canonbie or Wark
If you listen to the moorland air
You'll hear the faintest talk

Come on the wind when days are long
And the sky's a saffron glow
Reflections dark in pools of gold
The ghosts of riders show.

END NOTES

THE DOVECOTE
Speaking here as the dovecote itself. Now in ruins and supported by scaffolding but lacking funds for restoration, it stands deserted.

OXBRIDGE AND THEREABOUTS
'The Homes' Kids' refers to children from a set of homes in Oxbridge that looked after children who were in care.

KATIE
The portrait is how Katie looks now! She was only a baby when the poem was written.

THE MOAT FIELD
The garden of our house in Deighton bordered onto an ancient raised field surrounded by a moat. Its source is an eternal mystery!

THE TASK
A friend once remarked that no matter how technically advanced man becomes, even though we may eventually be able to make a bird, it would never be able to sing!

SWANS
Like swans, there are people who appear to glide along without a care but underneath they are paddling frantically.

THE CHRISTMAS CARD
I likened this special and apprehensive presentation of a Christmas card to the bringing of a gift by the Three Kings guided by a star.

SCARBOROUGH MEMORIES
Inset photographs from left to right:- Uncle Joe, Auntie Eth, Mam and Dad. Separate inset is me, aged about seven, with my double-barrelled gun.

GOODBYE

My next door neighbour and friend, Freda, because of her lovely Yorkshire accent, would always reply to something as being either "this 'ere" or "that there". So I devised a formula! If it was less than 15 feet away it was "this 'ere", a further distance would be "that there". It always made her laugh! This is captured in the painting.

THE BORDER REIVERS

Riding Names	:	The principal Reiver families.
Hobbler	:	Small sturdy horses sometimes called Galloways.
Steill	:	Steel
Jak	:	Sleeveless jacket made of padded material with small steel, iron or even bone plates woven into them.
Stave	:	Lance about 8ft. in length.
Hot trod	:	The right to legally pursue raiders / thieves of your goods in order to retrieve them. You could go anywhere carrying a burning torch on a lance. Anyone asked to join the pursuit had no choice by law but to do so.
March	:	The border was divided into three sections on either side. English East, Middle and West Marches and the same on the Scottish side. The Wardens were answerable to their own Monarchy.
Scumfishing	:	To break into fortified houses they would break down the main door, or 'Yett', on the ground floor and burn damp grass inside to smoke out the occupants of the rooms above the vaulted entrance room.
Pele and Bastle	:	Fortified houses
Days of Truce	:	When each Warden met his opposite number to account for all the murders and thefts. A truce was observed from sunrise to sunset.
Yett	:	Main door to a fortified house.
Spanish Morion	:	Steel helmet. Part of a reiver's armour.
Jeddart Justice	:	Execution without trial. Mass hangings of the main border reivers.
Corbie	:	Crow

Spur on a dinner plate:	In the case of some of the Reiver families, when the lady of the house produced a dinner plate at the table with just a single rider's spur upon it, it was telling the head of the house the larder was empty. It was an inference that a raid was required.
Salmon Cutting Redds:	In late autumn and early winter migrating salmon would be in the upper reaches of the River Liddle. They cut out a deep groove in the gravelled shallow river bed. The hen fish lays her eggs there and the cock fish fertilises them and covers them with the surrounding gravel to protect them from the winter floods.
The "Last Goodnight":	With the union of the crowns in 1603, James 1st of England and 6th of Scotland, put severe measures in place to crush the reivers and their way of life. This virtually put an end to their brutal regime, leaving only a few thieves to haunt the moors and waste lands of the Cheviots. These men were referred to as Moss Troopers.
Warden:	Generally speaking, The Warden was in overall charge of the defence of his March. In matters concerning the infringement of Border laws, he was in charge and held the power of life and death. He could order summary executions by beheading or hanging and was more often than not, in league with the subversive activities of the 'riding names' of his March.